Decode the Punch Line!

Each Hidden Pictures® puzzle in this book comes with a riddle.

Here's what you do:

1

Each hidden object to find corresponds to a letter.

2

Use the letters in the object code to solve the riddle.

3

Check the answers on pages 60–64 to see if you're correct!

Desert Drive

What can go for miles yet doesn't move?

A _ _ _ _ _

A	D	F	H	K	L
heart	star	ruler	glove	clock	sailboat

M	O	P	Q	R	Z
eyeglasses	toothbrush	saw	magnifying glass	teacup	sock

Art by Tim Davis

3

D1413206

Desert Drive

What can go for miles yet doesn't move?

___ ___ ___ ___ ___

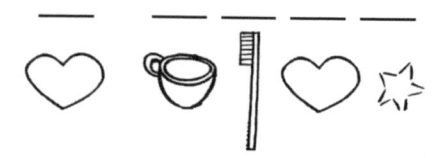

A	D	F	H	K	L
heart	star	ruler	glove	clock	sailboat

M	O	P	Q	R	Z
eyeglasses	toothbrush	saw	magnifying glass	teacup	sock

Art by Tim Davis

Shell Beach

What's the best day to go to the beach?

___ ___ ___ ___ ___ ___

A	B	D	E	G	I
mushroom	crown	arrow	bell	flashlight	wishbone

N	S	T	U	W	Y
needle	boot	ice-cream cone	toothbrush	slice of pizza	bowl

Art by Mary Sullivan

A Day at the Zoo

What keys are at the zoo?

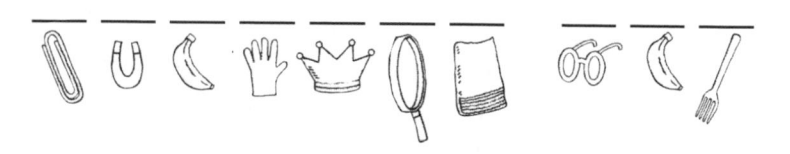

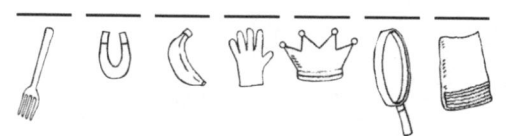

A	D	E	F	G	H
eyeglasses	fork	crown	arrow	rolling pin	crayon

K	M	N	O	S	Y
glove	paper clip	banana	magnet	book	magnifying glass

Art by Marilyn Janovitz

Takeoff

What did the pilot have for a snack?

A	**B**	**E**	**F**	**G**	**K**	**L**	**N**
propeller hat	boomerang	worm	golf club	olive	nail	crescent moon	green bean

O	**P**	**R**	**S**	**T**	**U**	**Y**
artist's pallette	snowman	game piece	flashlight	envelope	magnifying glass	slice of pie

Art by Scott Richie

Chilling by the Pool

Where do penguins like to go swimming?

A	C	E	H	K
tube of toothpaste	mitten	lemon	closed umbrella	key

L	M	O	P	S
banana	saltshaker	mushroom	clothespin	pennant

T	U	W	Y
pine tree	cherry	iron	yo-yo

Art by Laura Ferraro Close

The Ruff-ael Museum

What do you call a painting by a dog?

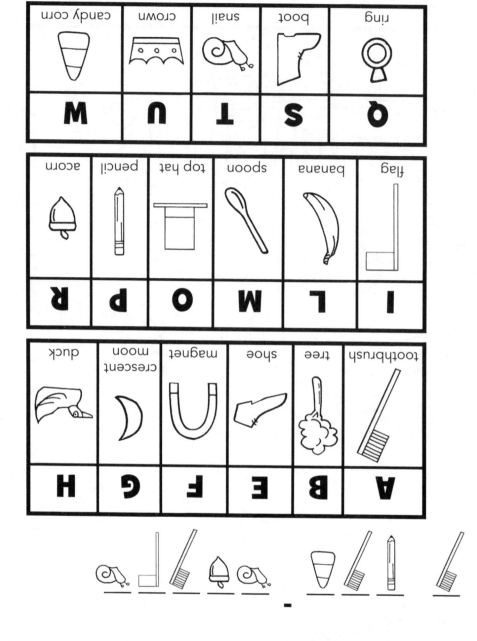

Art by Mike DeSantis

At the Camp Site

Why was the baseball player invited to go on the camping trip?

A	B	C	E	G	H	I
bowl	banana	toothbrush	candle	spoon	hockey stick	glove

M	N	O	P	R	S	T
artist's brush	lamp	shoe	lollipop	crayon	ice-cream cone	pennant

Art by Mary Sullivan

A-mouse-ment Park

What is small and has big ears and a trunk?

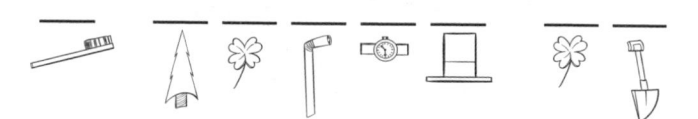

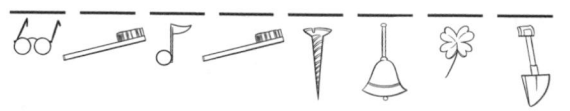

A	B	C	D	E	F	G	H
toothbrush	ladder	musical note	spool of thread	top hat	domino	flashlight	slice of pizza

I	J	K	L	M	N	O	P
handbell	drinking glass with straw	kite	needle	pine tree	shovel	four-leaf clover	golf club

Q	R	S	T	U	V	W
diamond	paper clip	wristwatch	screw	drinking straw	eyeglasses	spoon

CHEESE POPS

TICKETS

Art by Jennifer Harney

Ducky Day at the Beach

What time did the duck leave for the beach?

___ ___ ___ ___ ___ ___ ___ ___ ___ ___

___ ___ ___ ___ ___ ___

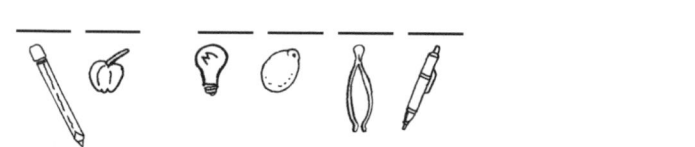

A	B	C	D	E	F	G	H
lemon	bowl	slice of bread	light bulb	crescent moon	cherry	Easter egg	fish

I	J	K	L	M	N	O
banana	toothbrush	measuring cup	needle	carrot	pen	pencil

P	Q	R	S	T	U	W
slice of pie	ring	rolling pin	yo-yo	star	wristwatch	wishbone

Art by Diana Zourelias

Aquarium Adventure

What is the best way to communicate with a fish?

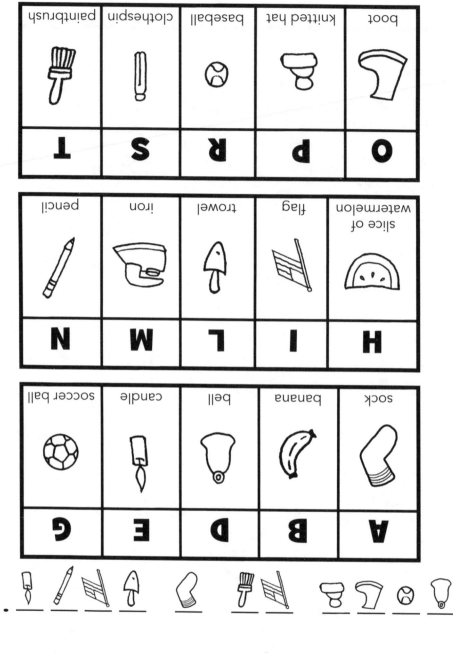

A sock	**B** banana	**D** bell	**E** candle	**G** soccer ball
H slice of watermelon	**I** flag	**L** trowel	**M** iron	**N** pencil
O boot	**P** knitted hat	**R** baseball	**S** clothespin	**T** paintbrush

Art by Patrick Girouard

Saddleback Canyon

Why do people ride horses?

O	R	S	T	V	Y
pencil	cinnamon bun	flag	paintbrush	cupcake	log

H	I	K	L	M	N
flashlight	ice-cream cone	boomerang	caterpillar	belt	banana

A	C	E	F	G
mug	knitted hat	mailbox	bird	ship

Art by Deborah Johnson

Now Boarding!

Where do chickens like to sit on a plane?

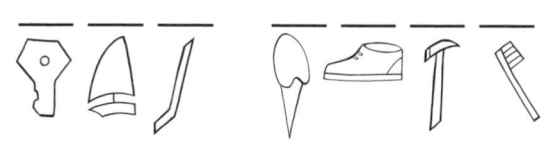

A	B	E	F	G	H
binoculars	shovel	hockey stick	book	toothbrush	sailboat

I	L	N	O	R	T	W
shoe	pencil	hammer	needle	comb	key	ice-cream cone

Art by Tim Davis

Anteaters' Picnic

Why don't anteaters ever get sick?

N	O	R	S	T	U	Y
tube of toothpaste	eyeglasses	needle and thread	hoe	pliers	sailboat	olive

A	B	D	E	F	H	I	L
paper clip	candle	mitten	magnet	screwdriver	funnel	light bulb	spool of thread

Art by Marilyn Janovitz

Dinosaur Discovery

Why do museums have old dinosaur bones?

A	B	C	D	E	F	H
puzzle piece	egg	heart	toothbrush	key	leaf	comb

I	M	N	O	P	R	S
wrench	kite	ice-cream cone	pencil	flag	ice-cream bar	snowman

T	U	V	W	X	Y	Z
candy cane	slice of pizza	ruler	drinking straw	snake	banana	baseball bat

Art by Jennifer Harney

Pig Pyramid

What do you call a pig who forgot to apply sunscreen?

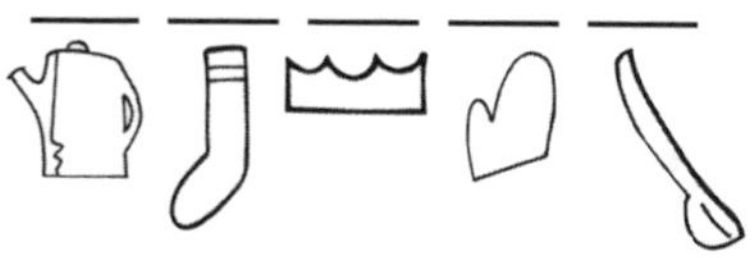

___ ___ ___ ___ ___

A	B	C	E	F
sock	pitcher	candle	banana	artist's brush

G	I	L	M	N
ladle	golf club	wishbone	crescent moon	spoon

O	P	Q	R	U	V	W
mitten	teacup	pencil	button	shoe	heart	bat

Art by Mike DeSantis

Feathered Friends

How do you find out the weather when you're on vacation?

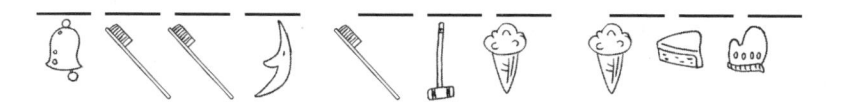

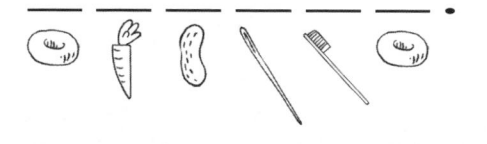

D	E	F	H	I	K
needle	mitten	artist's brush	slice of cake	carrot	crescent moon

L	M	N	O	T	U	W
bell	slice of pizza	peanut	toothbrush	ice-cream cone	croquet mallet	doughnut

Paddling on the Pond

How does a lion paddle his canoe?

__ __ __ __ __ __ __ __ __ __ __ __ __ .

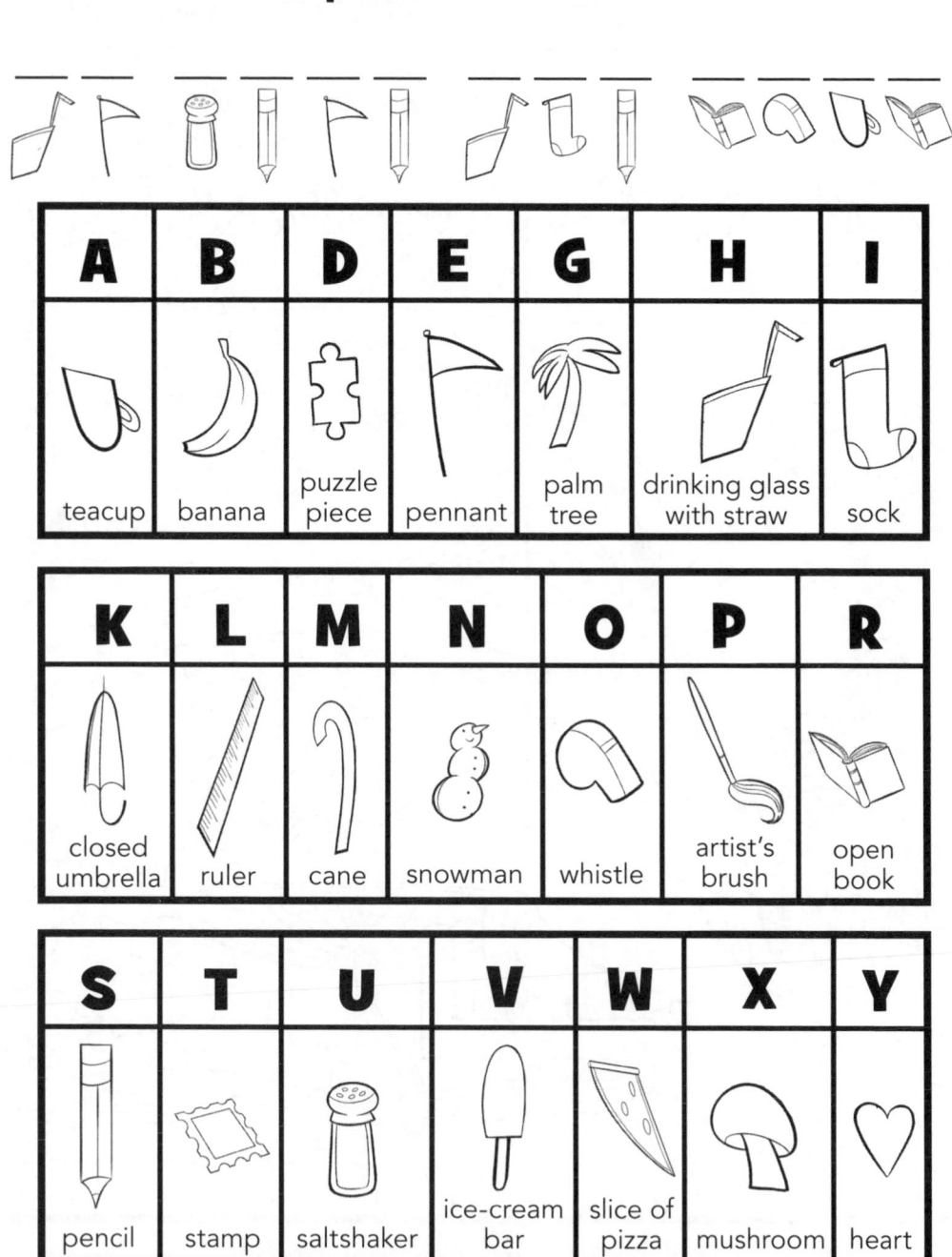

A	B	D	E	G	H	I
teacup	banana	puzzle piece	pennant	palm tree	drinking glass with straw	sock

K	L	M	N	O	P	R
closed umbrella	ruler	cane	snowman	whistle	artist's brush	open book

S	T	U	V	W	X	Y
pencil	stamp	saltshaker	ice-cream bar	slice of pizza	mushroom	heart

Art by Jennifer Harney

Snowmen on Skis

How do snowmen travel?

___ ___ ___ ___ ___ ___ ___

A	B	C	D	E
spoon	canoe	slice of pizza	crescent moon	ice-cream cone

G	H	I	K	L
mushroom	banana	crown	fish	needle

M	N	R	S	Y
pea pod	glove	drinking straw	eel	butter knife

Art by Gary Mohrman

Road Trip!

Where is the best place to eat while traveling?

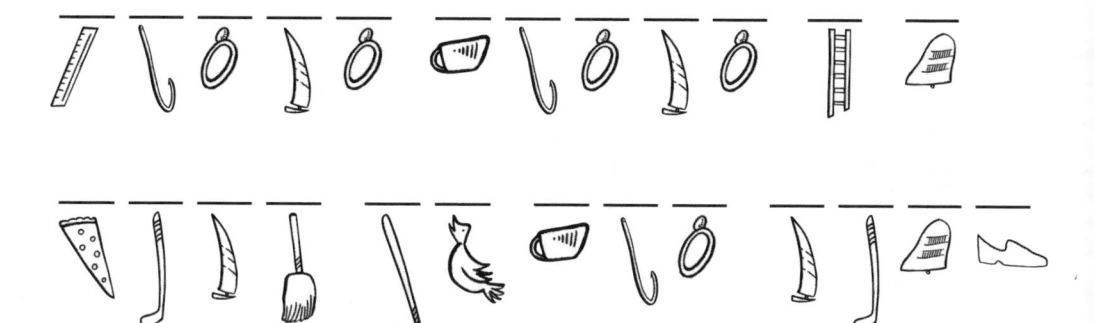

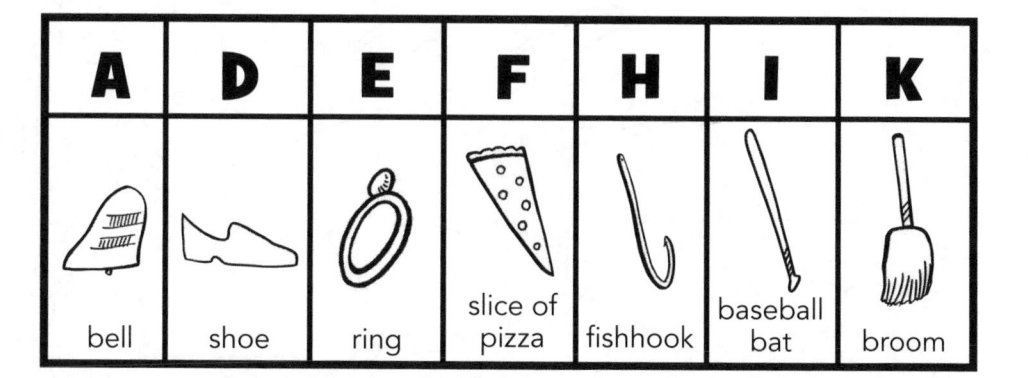

A	D	E	F	H	I	K
bell	shoe	ring	slice of pizza	fishhook	baseball bat	broom

N	O	R	S	T	W
bird	golf club	sailboat	ladder	teacup	ruler

Art by Karen Stormer Brooks

Birds in Flight

Why do birds fly south for the winter?

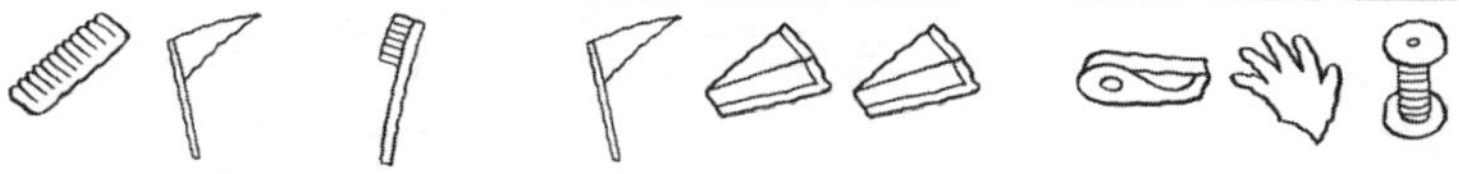

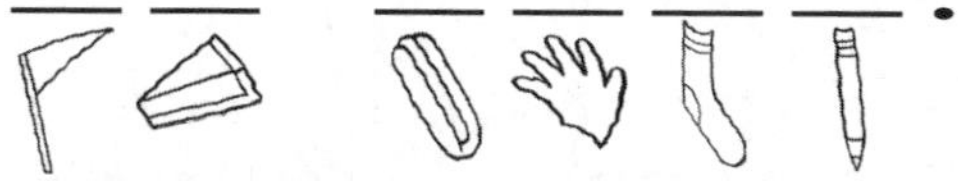

A	B	C	E	F	H	I
glove	bell	sailboat	envelope	tape dispenser	button	comb

K	L	M	N	O	P	Q
pencil	sock	drumstick	loaf of bread	slice of pie	spoon	golf club

R	S	T	U	W	Z
spool of thread	toothbrush	pennant	ruler	hot dog	ladle

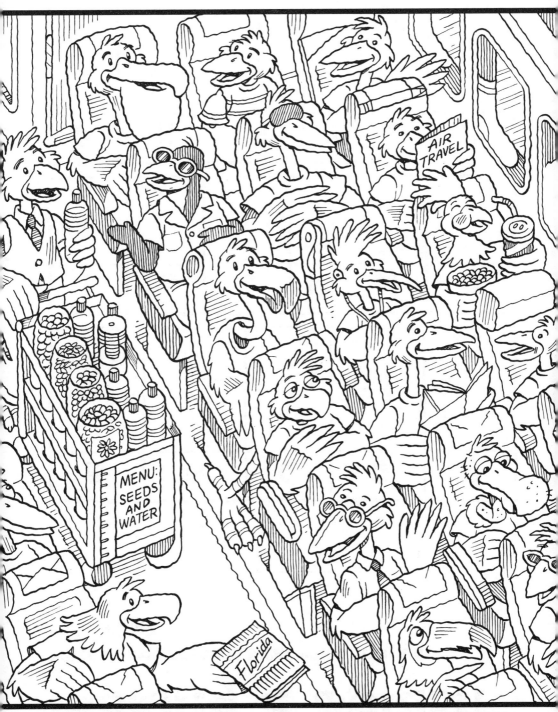

Art by David Helton

Making a Splash

What do zoo animals wear when they go swimming?

___ ___ ___ - ___ ___ ___ ___ ___ ___

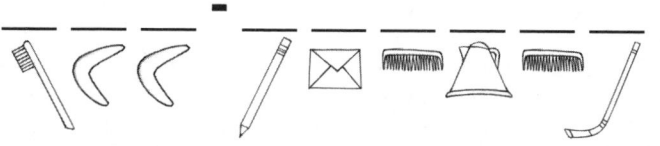

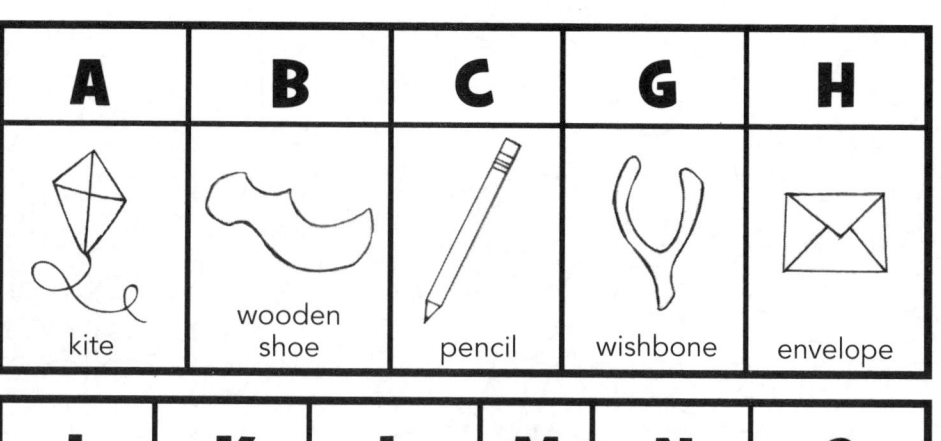

A	B	C	G	H
kite	wooden shoe	pencil	wishbone	envelope

I	K	L	M	N	O
comb	fried egg	bird	acorn	coffeepot	boomerang

P	R	S	T	U	Z
crowbar	baseball bat	hockey stick	pliers	scissors	toothbrush

The Welcom Inn

Art by Mark Corcoran

Around We Go

What did the horse say when the carousel ride was over?

" _ _ _ _ ."

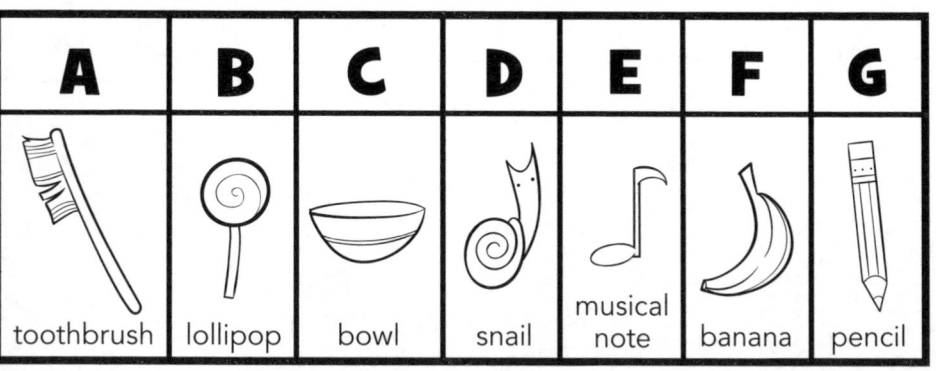

A	B	C	D	E	F	G
toothbrush	lollipop	bowl	snail	musical note	banana	pencil

H	I	L	M	N	O	P
fish	wristwatch	mushroom	crown	cupcake	tulip	handbell

Q	R	S	T	U	V	W
pine tree	artist's brush	dragonfly	traffic light	heart	candy cane	mug

Art by Jennifer Harney

Beach Read

What is more difficult than getting a hippo into a hammock?

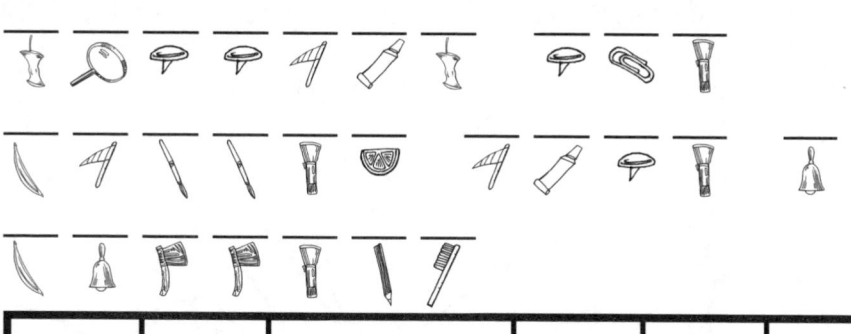

A	C	E	G	H	I
handbell	pencil	magnifying glass	apple core	banana	pennant

K	L	M	N	O	P
toothbrush	needle	hatchet	tube of toothpaste	flashlight	artist's brush

R	S	T	U	W
snake	wedge of orange	tack	ring	paper clip

Art by Maxim Mitrofanov

Nest Western

Where do birds stay when they're on vacation?

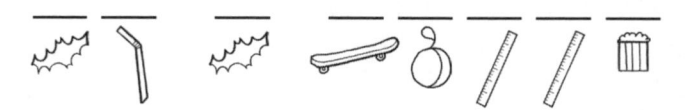

A	C	E	F	G	H
bat	skateboard	ruler	slice of cake	pencil	yo-yo

K	L	M	O	P	T
paintbrush	glove	cane	ice-cream cone	bag of popcorn	drinking straw

A Nice Day for a Hike

How do fleas travel from place to place?

__ __ __ __ __ __ __ __ - __ __ __ __ __ __

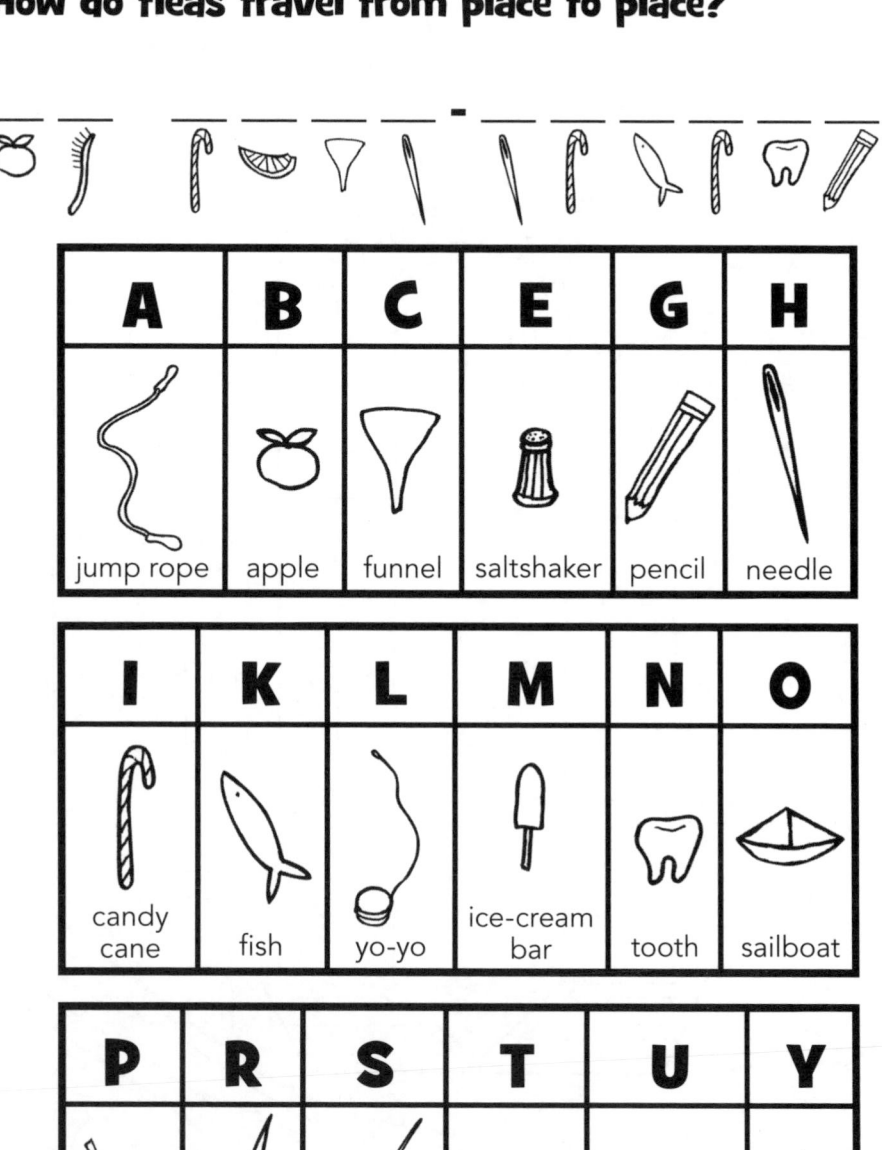

A	B	C	E	G	H
jump rope	apple	funnel	saltshaker	pencil	needle

I	K	L	M	N	O
candy cane	fish	yo-yo	ice-cream bar	tooth	sailboat

P	R	S	T	U	Y
spoon	artist's brush	lightning bolt	wedge of lemon	hamburger	brush

Art by Laura Ferraro Close

Dog's Day at the Dunes

Why didn't the dog go swimming at the beach?

A	**B**	**C**	**D**	**E**	**F**
sock	pointy hat	teacup	saltshaker	mitten	cherry

H	**M**	**N**	**O**	**P**	**R**
wishbone	baseball bat	pennant	pencil	high-heeled shoe	ruler

S	**T**	**U**	**V**	**W**	**Y**	**Z**
toothbrush	rabbit	fork	fishhook	carrot	nail	spoon

Art by Mike DeSantis

S'more Family Time

What happened when the silly camper bought a sleeping bag?

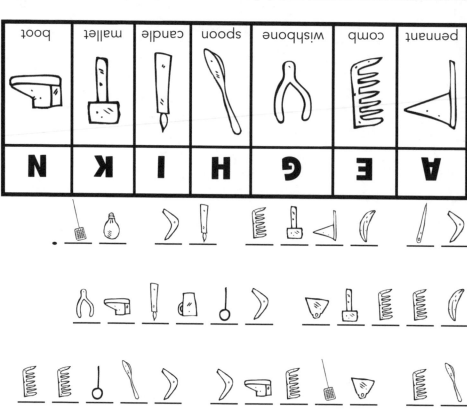

O	P	R	S	T	U	W	Y
needle	flyswatter	lollipop	bell	boomerang	light bulb	banana	mug

A	E	G	H	I	K	N
pennant	comb	wishbone	spoon	candle	mallet	boot

Art by Mary Sullivan

Desert Landscape

What is the best thing to take into the desert?

___ ___ ___ ___ ___ ___ ___ - ___ ___ ___ ___ ___

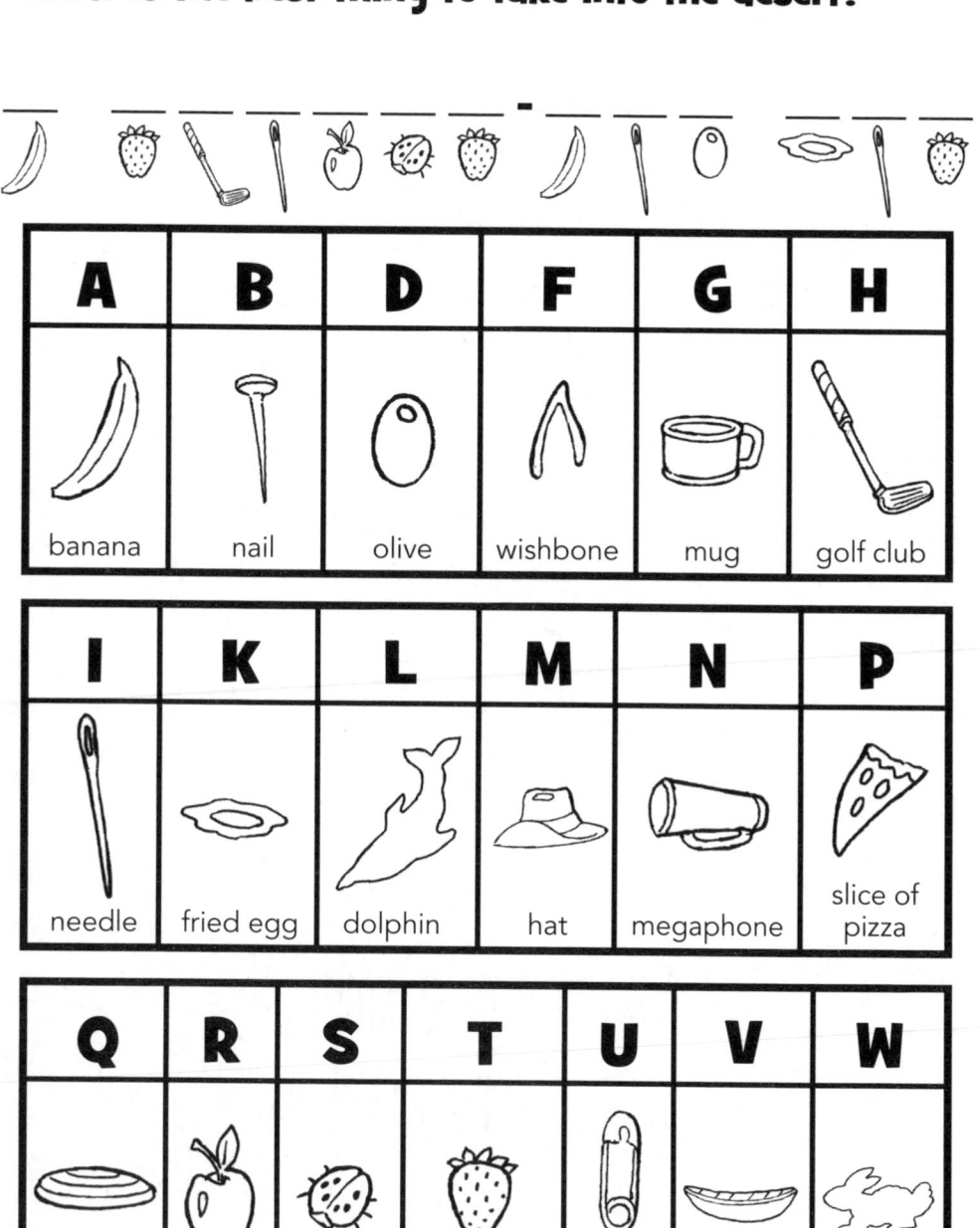

A	B	D	F	G	H
banana	nail	olive	wishbone	mug	golf club

I	K	L	M	N	P
needle	fried egg	dolphin	hat	megaphone	slice of pizza

Q	R	S	T	U	V	W
flying disk	apple	ladybug	strawberry	safety pin	canoe	rabbit

Art by Sherry Neidigh

Rockin' on the Road

What did the family listen to on the road trip?

___ ___ ___ - ___ ___ ___ ___ ___

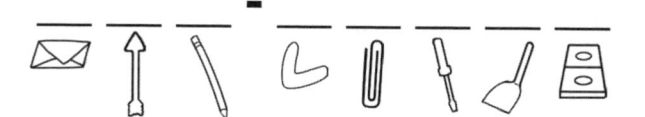

A	B	C	D	E	I	K
arrow	broccoli	envelope	potato	spatula	trowel	golf club

L	M	N	R	S	T	U
slice of pizza	pennant	screwdriver	pencil	domino	boomerang	paper clip

Art by Dana Regan

Answers

2–3 Desert Drive

What can go for miles yet doesn't move?

A ROAD

4–5 Shell Beach

What is the best day to go to the beach?

SUNDAY

6–7 A Day at the Zoo

What keys are at the zoo?

MONKEYS AND DONKEYS

8–9 Takeoff

What did the pilot have for a snack?

PLANE YOGURT

10–11 Chilling by the Pool

Where do penguins like to go swimming?

THE SOUTH POOL

12–13 The *Ruff*-ael Museum

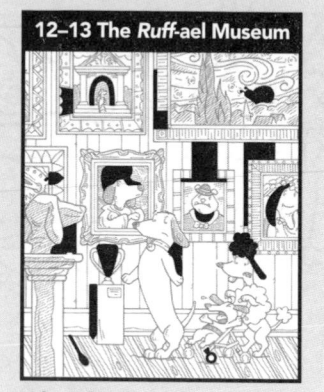

What do you call a painting by a dog?

A PAW-TRAIT

14–15 At the Camp Site

Why was the baseball player invited to go on the camping trip?
TO PITCH THE TENT

16–17 A-mouse-ment Park

What is small and has big ears and a trunk?
A MOUSE ON VACATION

18–19 Ducky Day at the Beach

What time did the duck leave for the beach?
AT THE QUACK OF DAWN

20–21 Aquarium Adventure

What is the best way to communicate with a fish?
DROP IT A LINE.

22–23 Saddleback Canyon

Why do people ride horses?
THEY'RE TOO HEAVY TO CARRY.

24–25 Now Boarding!

Where do chickens like to sit on a plane?
THE WING

Answers

26–27 Anteaters' Picnic

Why don't anteaters ever get sick?

THEY'RE FULL OF ANT-IBODIES.

28–29 Dinosaur Discovery

Why do museums have old dinosaur bones?

THEY CAN'T AFFORD NEW ONES.

30–31 Pig Pyramid

What do you call a pig who forgot to apply sunscreen?

BACON

32–33 Feathered Friends

How do you find out the weather when you're on vacation?

LOOK OUT THE WINDOW.

34–35 Paddling on the Pond

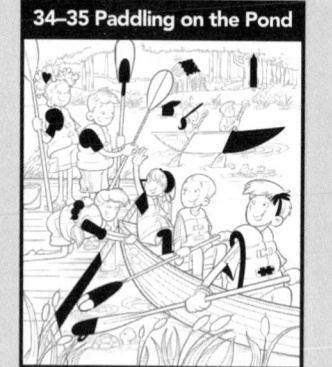

How does a lion paddle his canoe?

HE USES HIS ROAR.

36–37 Snowmen on Skis

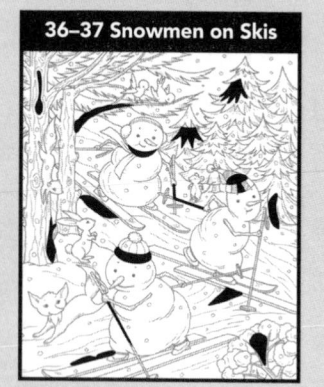

How do snowmen travel?

BY ICICLE

38–39 Road Trip!

Where is the best place to eat while traveling?
WHERE THERE'S A FORK IN THE ROAD

40–41 Birds in Flight

Why do birds fly south for the winter?
IT'S TOO FAR TO WALK.

42–43 Making a Splash

What do zoo animals wear when they go swimming?
ZOO-CCHINIS

44–45 Around We Go

What did the horse say when the carousel ride was over?
"WHOA."

46–47 Beach Read

What is more difficult than getting a hippo into a hammock?
GETTING TWO HIPPOS INTO A HAMMOCK

48–49 Nest Western

Where do birds stay when they're on vacation?
AT A CHEEP HOTEL

Answers

50–51 A Nice Day for a Hike

How do fleas travel from place to place?

BY ITCH-HIKING

52–53 Dog's Day at the Dunes

Why didn't the dog go swimming at the beach?

THE WAVES WERE TOO RUFF.

54–55 S'more Family Time

What happened when the silly camper bought a sleeping bag?

HE SPENT THREE WEEKS TRYING TO WAKE IT UP.

56–57 Desert Landscape

What is the best thing to take into the desert?

A THIRST-AID KIT

58–59 Rockin' on the Road

What did the family listen to on the road trip?

CAR-TUNES

Front Cover